HOMESCHOOL
Hours Log Book

HOMESCHOOL HOURS LOG BOOK

Name of School:

Years Covered:

Simple Guide

This Homeschool hours log book is designed according to **Missouri Homeschool Law** and helps you to log daily activities on week pages.

You can log both Core (away and home) and Non Core hours with ease. It's important to be organized by logging your homeschool hours.

Inside Feature

1. 53 Week homeschool planner-To document children studies.

2. Space to write Core hours and Non Core hours, total weekly hours, resource and books lists.

List of Books

List of Books

List of Books

List of Books

List of Books

List of Books

List of Books

List of Books

List of Books

List of Books

List of Resources

List of Resources

List of Resources

List of Resources

List of Resources

List of Resources

List of Resources

List of Resources

 # List of Resources

Week 1
Goals

Monday

Tuesday

Wednesday

Thursday

Core Hours (Home)	Core Hours (Away)
Non-Core Hours	Total Weekly Hours

Friday

Saturday

Sunday

Notes

Week 2

Goals

Monday

Tuesday

Wednesday

Thursday

Core Hours (Home)	Core Hours (Away)
Non-Core Hours	Total Weekly Hours

Friday

Saturday

Sunday

Notes

Week 3
Goals

Monday

Tuesday

Wednesday

Thursday

Core Hours (Home)	Core Hours (Away)
Non-Core Hours	Total Weekly Hours

Friday

Saturday

Sunday

Notes

Week 4

Goals

Monday

Tuesday

Wednesday

Thursday

Core Hours (Home)	Core Hours (Away)
Non-Core Hours	Total Weekly Hours

Friday

Saturday

Sunday

Notes

Week 5

Goals

Monday

Tuesday

Wednesday

Thursday

Core Hours (Home)	Core Hours (Away)
Non-Core Hours	Total Weekly Hours

Friday

Saturday

Sunday

Notes

Week 6

Goals

Monday

Tuesday

Wednesday

Thursday

Core Hours (Home)	Core Hours (Away)
Non-Core Hours	Total Weekly Hours

Friday

Saturday

Sunday

Notes

Week 7

Goals

Monday

Tuesday

Wednesday

Thursday

Core Hours (Home)	Core Hours (Away)
Non-Core Hours	Total Weekly Hours

Friday

Saturday

Sunday

Notes

Week 8

Goals

Monday

Tuesday

Wednesday

Thursday

Core Hours (Home)	Core Hours (Away)
Non-Core Hours	Total Weekly Hours

Friday

Saturday

Sunday

Notes

Week 9

Goals

Monday

Tuesday

Wednesday

Thursday

Core Hours (Home)	Core Hours (Away)
Non-Core Hours	Total Weekly Hours

Friday

Saturday

Sunday

Notes

 # Week 10

Goals

Monday

Tuesday

Wednesday

Thursday

Core Hours (Home)	Core Hours (Away)
Non-Core Hours	Total Weekly Hours

Friday

Saturday

Sunday

Notes

Week 11

Goals

Monday

Tuesday

Wednesday

Thursday

Core Hours (Home)	Core Hours (Away)
Non-Core Hours	Total Weekly Hours

Friday

Saturday

Sunday

Notes

Week 12

Goals

Monday

Tuesday

Wednesday

Thursday

Core Hours (Home)	Core Hours (Away)
Non-Core Hours	Total Weekly Hours

Friday

Saturday

Sunday

Notes

Week 13

Goals

Monday

Tuesday

Wednesday

Thursday

Core Hours (Home)	Core Hours (Away)
Non-Core Hours	Total Weekly Hours

Friday

Saturday

Sunday

Notes

Week 14

Goals

Monday

Tuesday

Wednesday

Thursday

Core Hours (Home)	Core Hours (Away)
Non-Core Hours	Total Weekly Hours

Friday

Saturday

Sunday

Notes

Week 15

Goals

Monday

Tuesday

Wednesday

Thursday

Core Hours (Home)	Core Hours (Away)
Non-Core Hours	Total Weekly Hours

Friday

Saturday

Sunday

Notes

Week 16

Goals

Monday

Tuesday

Wednesday

Thursday

Core Hours (Home)	Core Hours (Away)
Non-Core Hours	Total Weekly Hours

Friday

Saturday

Sunday

Notes

Week 17

Goals

Monday

Tuesday

Wednesday

Thursday

| Core Hours (Home) | Core Hours (Away) |
| Non-Core Hours | Total Weekly Hours |

Friday

Saturday

Sunday

Notes

Week 18

Goals

Monday

Tuesday

Wednesday

Thursday

Core Hours (Home)	Core Hours (Away)
Non-Core Hours	Total Weekly Hours

Friday

Saturday

Sunday

Notes

Week 19

Goals

Monday

Tuesday

Wednesday

Thursday

Core Hours (Home)	Core Hours (Away)
Non-Core Hours	Total Weekly Hours

Friday

Saturday

Sunday

Notes

Week 20

Goals

Monday

Tuesday

Wednesday

Thursday

Core Hours (Home)	Core Hours (Away)
Non-Core Hours	Total Weekly Hours

Friday

Saturday

Sunday

Notes

Week 21

Goals

Monday

Tuesday

Wednesday

Thursday

| Core Hours (Home) | Core Hours (Away) |
| Non-Core Hours | Total Weekly Hours |

Friday

Saturday

Sunday

Notes

Week 22

Goals

Monday

Tuesday

Wednesday

Thursday

Core Hours (Home)	Core Hours (Away)
Non-Core Hours	Total Weekly Hours

Friday

Saturday

Sunday

Notes

Week 23

Goals

Monday

Tuesday

Wednesday

Thursday

Core Hours (Home)	Core Hours (Away)
Non-Core Hours	Total Weekly Hours

Friday

Saturday

Sunday

Notes

Week 24

Goals

Monday

Tuesday

Wednesday

Thursday

Core Hours (Home)	Core Hours (Away)
Non-Core Hours	Total Weekly Hours

Friday

Saturday

Sunday

Notes

Week 25

Goals

Monday

Tuesday

Wednesday

Thursday

Core Hours (Home)	Core Hours (Away)
Non-Core Hours	Total Weekly Hours

Friday

Saturday

Sunday

Notes

Week 26

Goals

Monday

Tuesday

Wednesday

Thursday

Core Hours (Home)	Core Hours (Away)
Non-Core Hours	Total Weekly Hours

Friday

Saturday

Sunday

Notes

Week 27

Goals

Monday

Tuesday

Wednesday

Thursday

Core Hours (Home)	Core Hours (Away)
Non-Core Hours	Total Weekly Hours

Friday

Saturday

Sunday

Notes

Week 28

Goals

Monday

Tuesday

Wednesday

Thursday

| Core Hours (Home) | Core Hours (Away) |
| Non-Core Hours | Total Weekly Hours |

Friday

Saturday

Sunday

Notes

Week 29

Goals

Monday

Tuesday

Wednesday

Thursday

Core Hours (Home)	Core Hours (Away)
Non-Core Hours	Total Weekly Hours

Friday

Saturday

Sunday

Notes

Week 30

Goals

Monday

Tuesday

Wednesday

Thursday

| Core Hours (Home) | Core Hours (Away) |
| Non-Core Hours | Total Weekly Hours |

Friday

Saturday

Sunday

Notes

Week 31

Goals

Monday

Tuesday

Wednesday

Thursday

Core Hours (Home)	Core Hours (Away)
Non-Core Hours	Total Weekly Hours

Friday

Saturday

Sunday

Notes

Week 32

Goals

Monday

Tuesday

Wednesday

Thursday

| Core Hours (Home) | Core Hours (Away) |
| Non-Core Hours | Total Weekly Hours |

Friday

Saturday

Sunday

Notes

Week 33

Goals

Monday

Tuesday

Wednesday

Thursday

Core Hours (Home)	Core Hours (Away)
Non-Core Hours	Total Weekly Hours

Friday

Saturday

Sunday

Notes

Week 34

Goals

Monday

Tuesday

Wednesday

Thursday

| Core Hours (Home) | Core Hours (Away) |
| Non-Core Hours | Total Weekly Hours |

Friday

Saturday

Sunday

Notes

Week 35

Goals

Monday

Tuesday

Wednesday

Thursday

Core Hours (Home)	Core Hours (Away)
Non-Core Hours	Total Weekly Hours

Friday

Saturday

Sunday

Notes

Week 36

Goals

Monday

Tuesday

Wednesday

Thursday

| Core Hours (Home) | Core Hours (Away) |
| Non-Core Hours | Total Weekly Hours |

Friday

Saturday

Sunday

Notes

Week 37

Goals

Monday

Tuesday

Wednesday

Thursday

| Core Hours (Home) | Core Hours (Away) |
| Non-Core Hours | Total Weekly Hours |

Friday

Saturday

Sunday

Notes

Week 38

Goals

Monday

Tuesday

Wednesday

Thursday

Core Hours (Home)	Core Hours (Away)
Non-Core Hours	Total Weekly Hours

Friday

Saturday

Sunday

Notes

Week 39

Goals

Monday

Tuesday

Wednesday

Thursday

Core Hours (Home)	Core Hours (Away)
Non-Core Hours	Total Weekly Hours

Friday

Saturday

Sunday

Notes

Week 40

Goals

Monday

Tuesday

Wednesday

Thursday

Core Hours (Home)	Core Hours (Away)
Non-Core Hours	Total Weekly Hours

Friday

Saturday

Sunday

Notes

Week 41

Goals

Monday

Tuesday

Wednesday

Thursday

Core Hours (Home)	Core Hours (Away)
Non-Core Hours	Total Weekly Hours

Friday

Saturday

Sunday

Notes

Week 42

Goals

Monday

Tuesday

Wednesday

Thursday

Core Hours (Home)	Core Hours (Away)
Non-Core Hours	Total Weekly Hours

Friday

Saturday

Sunday

Notes

Week 43

Goals

Monday

Tuesday

Wednesday

Thursday

Core Hours (Home)	Core Hours (Away)
Non-Core Hours	Total Weekly Hours

Friday

Saturday

Sunday

Notes

Week 44

Goals

Monday

Tuesday

Wednesday

Thursday

Core Hours (Home)	Core Hours (Away)
Non-Core Hours	Total Weekly Hours

Friday

Saturday

Sunday

Notes

Week 45

Goals

Monday

Tuesday

Wednesday

Thursday

Core Hours (Home)	Core Hours (Away)
Non-Core Hours	Total Weekly Hours

Friday

Saturday

Sunday

Notes

Week 46

Goals

Monday

Tuesday

Wednesday

Thursday

Core Hours (Home)	Core Hours (Away)
Non-Core Hours	Total Weekly Hours

Friday

Saturday

Sunday

Notes

Week 47

Goals

Monday

Tuesday

Wednesday

Thursday

Core Hours (Home)	Core Hours (Away)
Non-Core Hours	Total Weekly Hours

Friday

Saturday

Sunday

Notes

Week 48

Goals

Monday

Tuesday

Wednesday

Thursday

Core Hours (Home)	Core Hours (Away)
Non-Core Hours	Total Weekly Hours

Friday

Saturday

Sunday

Notes

Week 49

Goals

Monday

Tuesday

Wednesday

Thursday

| Core Hours (Home) | Core Hours (Away) |
| Non-Core Hours | Total Weekly Hours |

Friday

Saturday

Sunday

Notes

Week 50

Goals

Monday

Tuesday

Wednesday

Thursday

Core Hours (Home)	Core Hours (Away)
Non-Core Hours	Total Weekly Hours

Friday

Saturday

Sunday

Notes

Week 51

Goals

Monday

Tuesday

Wednesday

Thursday

Core Hours (Home)	Core Hours (Away)
Non-Core Hours	Total Weekly Hours

Friday

Saturday

Sunday

Notes

Week 52

Goals

Monday

Tuesday

Wednesday

Thursday

Core Hours (Home)	Core Hours (Away)
Non-Core Hours	Total Weekly Hours

Friday

Saturday

Sunday

Notes

Week 53

Goals

Monday

Tuesday

Wednesday

Thursday

Core Hours (Home)	Core Hours (Away)
Non-Core Hours	Total Weekly Hours

Friday

Saturday

Sunday

Notes

Thank you
for purchasing
from us

Made in the USA
Monee, IL
11 July 2022